FREE
AIR

FREE
AIR

poems

JOE WENKE

trans
über

Stamford, Connecticut 2014

Trans Über LLC
www.transuber.com

To reach the author or Trans Über email:
joewenke@joewenke.org

ISBN: 978-0-9907022-1-4

Digital editions available.

Manufactured in the United States of America
First Edition

FRONTISPIECE: JOY BROWN

DESIGN AND COMPOSITION: JOHN LOTTE/BLUE MOUNTAIN MARKETING

www.joewenke.org
Follow Joe Wenke on Twitter @joewenke.

for Mark, Ryan, Olivia and Gisele

contents

I Talk When You Talk *1*

I Think Without Thinking *2*

Bone on the Sand *3*

Lament of an Old Man *4*

Self-Diagnosis *5*

The Heater *6*

I Hate Everybody *7*

Nothing's Free *8*

The Religious Right *10*

Penetralia *11*

The Final Act *12*

Revelation at Pompei *13*

I Like to Lie *14*

Spontaneous Erection *15*

I Used to Drive My Car *16*

What Was I Thinking? *17*

I Feel Guilty *18*

Bright Green Eyes *19*

Immortality *20*

Sustenance *21*

Free Air *22*

Do the Opposite! *23*

Out to Lunch *24*

The End *25*

Sipping Iced Tea on My Patio *26*

At a Party in Media *27*

The Magic of Creation 28

Cool Fool 29

Our Love 31

You Are the Queen 32

Star Stuff 33

Therapy Dog 35

Loner 36

Autumn Tree 37

The Undying Image 38

Song 39

Big Butt 40

Down Here 41

What's the Difference? 42

I Hate Holidays 44

The Hypocrite 45

Am I Depressed? 46

Headphones 47

Love's Revelation 49

The Golden Age 50

The Yawn 51

Family Restaurant 52

The Nanny 53

Handyman Special 54

Waiting 55

FREE
AIR

I Talk When You Talk

I talk when you talk.
When you're silent,
I'm silent too.
It's what I do.
I can't help myself.
I try,
but it doesn't work.
I can't lie.
We get along just fine
when we're apart.
When I think of you,
it breaks my heart.
I forget.
Why did we ever get together?
I forget.
What was it like to be in love?
I forget.
Then I remember.
At this point
it doesn't matter.
There's nothing
we can do.
I talk when you talk.
When you're silent,
I'm silent too.

I Think Without Thinking

I think without thinking.
My brain does all the work,
keeping its secrets from me.
Only later do I discover
what I already know.
The timing is a mystery.
If only I knew then
what I know now,
but I didn't,
and I don't.
I don't know
what I don't know,
and I don't know
what I do know.
I don't know what to do,
but I know my brain will tell me later.

Bone on the Sand

I feel like a bone
carried and cleaned
by the ocean,
dried by the sun,
left to bleach alone,
so smooth and
hollow inside,
while on the sand
not a footprint
can be found.

Lament of an Old Man

What sadness!
I am at the end
of my life.
I realize this today
for the first time.
It has been with me
all morning.
Even now as I watch
the day settle in,
I know my life
is over.
And to think,
I was just beginning
to get the hang of it.

Self-Diagnosis

I got the heebie-jeebies.
I got the shivers and the shakes.
I got Benign Positional Vertigo.
I got a penchant for mistakes.

I got tingles in my lower legs.
I got tangles in my hair.
I got an ENT with ADHD
I'm OCD, so there!

I got tinnitus and dizziness.
I'm going deaf in my right ear.
They torture but won't kill me,
the symptoms of Meniere's.

The malady that quashes me
has yet to be disclosed.
When I know which one, I'll be done
with nothing else to diagnose.

The Heater

It rumbles on
for hours and hours,
and I never even hear it,
the heater in my apartment,
old machinery, old iron and dust,
squeaking metal and chipped blue paint.
It rumbles on
for days and days,
unheard and unattended,
until it all shuts down.
The cold inevitable gasp
of metal letting up,
and it all shuts down.
The room shuts down,
and then I hear it:
The silence rushes in
that has been rumbling on
for days and days,
for weeks
been building up.
The heater, locked inside a closet,
squeaking metal and chipped blue paint
and the dust upon the floor.
Then it all shuts down.

I Hate Everybody

I hate everybody
except you
and my children.
For me it's over
with "Hi, how are you doing?"
It's really true.
I cut people off
immediately.
I see their limitations
and move on.
I hardly arrive,
and I'm already gone.
In my beginning is my end
and yours as well, my friend.
We're done.
There's nothing more
to say.

Nothing's Free

Nothing's free.
My will's not free.
I'm not the executor.
My brain makes all the decisions
for me.
I don't count.
Later on
I find out
what the hell I'm up to.

Nothing's free.
All the girls I know charge
for freebies.
I'm happy to pay,
but freebies used to be free.
Now it's a product or a service
with no guarantee,
and they charge you more
for GFE,
even more than that
for VIP.
Things ain't what they used to be.
They never were.
Honey in the beehive,
honey bun,
but it'll cost you
plenty
to be that one.

You wanna be free?
Think again.
Better yet,
ask your brain.
Your brain will tell you.
It's in charge.
And that's the beginning
and the end
of freedom.

The Religious Right

The religious right
is so uptight.
They hate on the gay
every day.
Don't they have something else to say
like love thy neighbor
or do not judge?
No matter what
they just won't budge.
A man loves a man.
But that's not part
of God's perfect plan.
That's what they say.
But don't blame them.
God is the one
who's anti-gay.
That's their story.
That's their power
and their glory.
They're not bigots.
They just know that
hate is the ticket
that will get them
through heaven's gate.

Penetralia

The ceaseless cries of night birds
cannot be understood.
The blackness of the wood,
its mystery beyond words,
yields nothing to the eye.
Still my mind broods on obsessed
when these dark forms appear.
Some truth seems always near.
Are people base or blessed?
Is spirit but a lie?
Whether nothing be confessed
or something more, I fear
the ceaseless cries of night birds,
the blackness of the wood.

The Final Act

Tonight the sky is dark.
The clouds contain the stars,
obscured themselves
by constellations of blackness
without origin.
Down to distances
measurable by the imagination,
space is shrunken.
Nothing moves throughout the world
except one mind,
limited and fallible.
Yet I believe that I can see
that what seem to be
the icy points of branches
black together with the blackness
of the sky
make one dimension
that reveals all existence
as clearly as if the light
that moved the sun and stars
had, before expiring,
illuminated all creation
in one final act of love.

Revelation at Pompei

Only the final expression endures
bearing the weight of centuries
cast in stone:
A man with a look of amazed despair,
volcanic madness burying
everything about him,
is sitting, straining
toward his wife and children,
trying to embrace
though he cannot save them
in one last fleeting look of love.

I Like to Lie

I like to lie.
I lie a lot.
I lie just to keep in practice.
It might be important,
or it might not.
It's all the same to me.
Lying sets me free —
from my girlfriend,
from my wife,
from my boss,
from my life.
I say whatever suits me,
whatever comes to mind.
I'll be true to you forever.
Yada, yada, yada.
The money's in the bank.
Blah, blah, blah, blah, blah, blah.
Lying is my SOP, my MO and my praxis.
The only thing that's better?
Cheating on my taxes.

Spontaneous Erection

It's been at least a week
since I had a spontaneous erection.
I can't remember the last time
I kissed a girl.
Ice cream?
I never eat it.
I used to play tennis
all the time,
but now I don't even own a racket.
I read a lot
but remember nothing.
When I lose my place,
I just give up.
I would do crossword puzzles
all the time
if I knew some of the answers.
Whenever I ask for directions,
I don't listen.
I have no idea what I'm doing next.
I keep my iPod
permanently on shuffle.
I keep my dreams and schemes
on hold.
I'd like to know
if this is just me.
Am I the only one?
Does anybody else
feel this way?

I Used to Drive My Car

I used to drive my car,
but now my car drives me
everywhere.
It's just so easy and free.
I know it's against the law,
but I don't care.
I sit in the back,
and off we go
wherever I say —
to the market,
to the show,
to the strip club,
to the bank.
What if the people laugh?
What if the people stare?
I love my car!
my car —
the perfect chauffeur!

What Was I Thinking?

What was I thinking?
You never said you loved me,
not even once,
and you hated yourself
for hating me.
When you died,
I checked the email account
I had set up especially for you,
and there it was,
the final communication.
There was nothing new.

I Feel Guilty

I feel guilty all the time,
but I've never committed a single crime.
I don't cheat.
I don't steal.
I don't eat
in between meals.
I don't gossip.
I don't slander.
I don't pimp.
I don't pander.
I don't curse.
I don't swear.
I've never done anything
to anybody anywhere.

I was told when I was a kid
that being born was what I did.
That was my one and only crime
at that time.

Then I hit puberty
and wanted to fuck.
That's when my brain
really got stuck.

Wanting to fuck?
That's a crime?
So that's when I started
feeling guilty all the time.

Bright Green Eyes

Have you seen through the night
bright green eyes,
as far away as stars,
as cold as the white cornea
light of cold lost years in space,
close as my imagination bright,
warm as the starry morning?
Yes, I know that she would love me
if only she could know me,
but do you know
how lost and futile
are the bright green eyes,
they are so beautiful,
and the thought that they are seeing
through the night
bright green eyes,
as far away as stars,
as close as my imagination bright,
waiting through the night
to fall toward their love?

Immortality

If mankind lives another million years,
if millions of millennia be subsumed within a second,
is Shakespeare doomed to shape a jot of hieroglyphics
and Christ to be consumed by a ravenous instant
to waste in the obscurity of Nous?

Sustenance

We are sustained
by small benignities,
though the pain that they betray
inside the unseen core of the body
confirms the fear of isolation,
the utter terror of an end
without a single lover.
Not family or friends
or the familiarity of places
can ever touch the heart —
the heart we barely can imagine,
knowing nothing sure about it —
except that it is beating as a space
and existing as an absence
that does not stop.

Free Air

Nothing's better than free air.
You can breathe it anywhere
you are.
Fill your lungs.
Look up at the sky.
You got the sun.
The wind is blowing.
Why ask why?
You know you'll die
some day,
but right now
the air is feeling fine.
It's free.
I'll say it again.
The air is free!
Nobody cares
about anything,
not even me.
I'm glad.
Nobody's asking why.

Do the Opposite!

I used to walk a straight line,
but now I walk it crooked.
I used to hit the ball fair,
but now I try to hook it.

I'm inside out.
I'm upside down.
My phone is off.
I'm out of town.
I'm on the move.
I'm good to go.
I'm full of gas.
Do you want to know
my next move?
It's the opposite.

Out to Lunch

I'm out to lunch.
I'm under construction.
I'm under new management.
To be continued.
A work in progress.
Indefinitely on hold.

I have no ETA.
I have no SOP.
I have no ROI.
I'm ADBB.

The End

Some people leave
when they see it coming.
Some people stay
long after it's come.
Some people never know
that it happened.
The end.
It's over.
Finished.
Gone.

Sipping Iced Tea on My Patio

On such a peaceful day as this
I might almost believe
that this same bright sun
could not shine
upon the bloated body
of a child
starving in Somalia.
This same green grass
could not conceal the gun
of an assassin in Fort Wayne.

At a Party in Media

The look upon my friend
with his fingers extended
as he approached the other's side
and touched her
was subtle as the lowering tide.
I say
there was nothing
it resembled more
than the last green waves of ocean
stretching out against the shore,
and his body's shape as they danced
in motion close to shaking
was nearer the truth,
all desire laid bare,
than the last leaf of autumn hanging.

The Magic of Creation

I no longer think
of the world as magical.
At night banalities soften
but do not disappear.
When I close my eyes,
I hear no dance of voices
in the leaves.
I sense no glad improvisation
in the instant that I wink.
I am certain, for example,
that there is no mustache
penciled on God's face
that, just as my eyes are opening,
must be hurriedly erased.
No, I do not search suspiciously
for the most subtle trace of a smile
as the wind moves indifferently
through the leaves upon the street.
Yet, having spoken, I feel foolish,
the tragic turned banal satirical.
My sorrow seems too serious,
my honesty indiscreet,
though no less honest in its fault.
I force a smile at my own futility
and note a sort of magic after all.

Cool Fool

I'm a cool fool
What's that

I do what I want
I know where it's at

I don't have to think
I know what to do

I go with the flow
I roll with the crew

I don't need to click
I don't need to clack

I don't play the field
I don't watch my back

I don't need to flip
I don't need to flop

I don't need to bip
I don't need to bop

I know what is real
I know what is fake

I know when to boil
I know when to bake

I know when to walk
I know when to run

I know when to start
I know when I'm done

I know who's a friend
I know who's a foe

I know when to come
I know when to go

I don't need a stick
I don't need a stone

I don't need a break
I don't need a loan

I don't need a horse
I don't need a mule

I don't need no plan
I'm a cool fool

Our Love

Our love is like the universe,
infinite and expanding,
profound as the curvature of space,
radiant as a billion rising suns,
a quantum reality,
eternally new,
beyond reason and science.
Our love
we know is true.

You Are the Queen

You are the queen of the universe
Self-created and elusive
Brilliant and dark
Deep and mysterious
Both particle and wave
Both here and there
The breath of inspiration
The dreamer of truths
The mistress of change
The face of eternity
Forever my love.

Star Stuff

For Lori, February 1985

The nitrogen in our DNA, the calcium in our teeth,
the iron in our blood . . . was made in the interior of
collapsing stars. We are made of star stuff. —*Carl Sagan*

— 1 —

Billions of years ago,
millions of light years away,
we made a pact inside a star
to meet again.
Was it that distant memory,
a sweet explosion of wills,
that brightened your face
as you turned
to meet me again?

— 2 —

I've waited for you, my love,
in all the familiar, desolate places,
in train stations, bus stations, airports
and apartments.
I've waited for your return
from New York City, Hartford, Boston
and Rome.
I've waited across the vacuum of space,
across the emptiness of our former lives,
across distances beyond all
but our imaginations.

I've waited through the creation
and the destruction of worlds,
through the loss of all
but the promise of love,
waiting from darkness to darkness
in the knowledge
that I would find you again,
delicate as stardust,
beautiful as light.
I've waited for you
as you've waited for me,
waiting from the moment of goodbye,
waiting from the wave beyond the window,
cherishing the precious touch that slips away,
the long, sad smile that disappears
until we meet again.

Therapy Dog

He's sitting on my lap.
Then he takes a crap
on the floor.
Still he's better behaved
than my ex-boyfriend.
One day
he sat on my lap
for about an hour and a half.
Then he got up
and walked out the door.
That was the last time
I saw him.

Loner

When I'm not with you,
all I do is work
and think of you,
waiting for your call
or your text,
waiting for what's next.

I do whatever's necessary
and nothing more.
Nothing less.
I eat and drink
and stay healthy.
I exercise
a little.
I stay fit,
sort of.
I'm not a mess,
but I'm not right.
I pretend
to be sociable,
but I'm not.
It's just another form
of work,
while I wait for you,
for your call
or for your text,
waiting for what's next.

Autumn Tree

A tree flames
beside the parking lot,
which throughout the summer
had stood invisible,
hidden in green leaves
and the light of noon,
not even the black bark
was taken seriously.
Someone must have set
a fire in the night!
At the top
bare branches go out
and cut the sky.

The Undying Image

On a winding path
through snow dusted weeds,
rooted sticks that shake
with every motion
of the February wind
now motionless
in momentary pause,
I look upon
a lifeless sparrow
frozen to stone.
And I see
that when imagination,
the great preserver and resemblancer,
is fixed upon the form of death,
it is the image of mortality
that does not die
and rises out of darkness
to deny the chance of sleep.

Song

I remember
running from a wave,
so big a wave
it seemed to a child of four
to be twice as big as it was
like a scary fairy tale dragon
or the nightmare dreams
of a later age,
blank seas that frighten
and never awaken.

I reached the shore relieved of my awe
and turned to see
the wave no longer rushing after me.
I should have walked into that wave.
Then it might not have disappeared.
I might have found a deeper shore
and through the wave have heard the sounds
of children singing by the sea
or maybe even sung myself.

Big Butt

Big butt.
Big butted.
Big butt.
Big butted.
She's dancing up a storm,
transgressing all the norms.
Big butt.
Big butted.
Big butt.
Big butted.

Down Here

There's nothing going on
down here
There's nothing going on
down here
I'm polishing my knees
struggling to please
There's nothing gong on
down here.

It's been this way
since the beginning
of time
Being poor is the greatest crime
Being poor is the oldest joke
You get no respect
when you're always broke
You get no respect
when you're in the hole
You get no respect
when you lick the bowl.

There's nothing going on
down here
There's nothing going on
down here
I'm polishing my knees
struggling to please
There's nothing gong on
down here.

What's the Difference?

When everybody's one way
and you're the other —
You're not like your father
You're not like your mother
You're not like anybody else
in your family —
You become the outsider.
It could be anything —
Politics
Religion
Education
Money
They're cis.
You're trans.
They're straight.
You're gay.
They all stayed home.
You moved away.
Whatever —
You're the one
they have to excuse.
You're the one
who's going to lose.
You're the one
who could have been great.
You're the one
they love and hate.

You're the one
who won't go along.
You're the one
who's always wrong.
You're the one
who's different.

I Hate Holidays

I hate holidays.
Everything's closed,
and there's nothing to do
except spend time with family
and others who supposedly love
or like you.

The Hypocrite

I say one thing
and do another.
That's my MO.
I say yes
when I mean no.
I say stay
when I mean go.
I say I'll always be true
right after I cheat.
I say it with a smile.
I don't miss a beat,
and I mean it.
I am —
true to myself, that is,
true to the way
I need to play this game,
because I'm playing this game
to win.

Am I Depressed?

Am I depressed
or just really sad?
I can't tell the difference.
What's the definition?
Is it based
on how bad you feel
or how often
you feel bad?
What if
it's going on
every minute
of every day
even when you're sleeping?
Does that mean you're depressed?
What does it take
to qualify for medication?
What's that old expression?
Oh, yeah,
about weeping
and gnashing of teeth —
Suppose I'm just fed up
with everybody
and everything.
What's that called?
And what if I don't care anyway?
What's that?
Does that mean I'm depressed?

Headphones

The music circles my head,
an unseen light,
encircling, enclosed,
I am protected.
There is an aura
in my dark room,
rising in the air,
the haunted,
deepening air.
Music circles my head,
the yellow green light
of the moon,
rising in the air
in my room,
dark and deepening.
Upon the yellow green dirt
of the moon
I lie,
my body
loose and free
inside the circle of the moon,
so close, so pure,
so private.
Let the circle
be the world,
the music moving in the air,
an unseen light.
We break it open!
And you and I and we
infuse, enter each other,
the world.

We break it open!
And there is a depth
to the world
inside the motionless whir
of the world,
in nature,
now, the crickets
and the deep dark night.
We break it open!
And there is a depth
to the world
inside
where there is
no inside.
There are no boundaries,
loose and free,
and the world and you and I,
and now —
the music circles my head,
an unseen light encircling,
enclosed.
I am protected.
There is an aura
in my dark room,
rising in the air,
the music,
moving in the air,
an unseen light.
We break it open!

Love's Revelation

For Lori

Once you were the horizon's edge,
neither sea nor sky,
neither land's end
nor its beginning,
but the isolated soul's projection
of reality,
receding before its grasp,
a silent apparition,
becoming now more
now less real
by its constancy of motion,
by its fixity in the mind.

And now you lie beside me,
close as our next embrace,
warm as tomorrow's memory,
new as the revelation
of love awakening at dawn.

The Golden Age

Was there ever one moment
in this whole exhausting sorrowing history
that is human
when a girl and a boy,
unaware of meaning
and unrestrained by risk,
opened their eyes upon a world
contained by their embrace
and impressed it with a kiss?

If there was,
then our lost hope
was begotten by love,
and it was then
that the loss was first known.

The Yawn

In the absence
of any object of interest
the mind turns to itself,
and, finding the nullity within
in harmony with
the nullity without,
orders the mouth
to open
upon a perfect world
devoid of doubt.

Family Restaurant

Let's see if I have the concept right.
You poison yourself,
while kids scream and fight.
You wait to get seated
in a long line too
because you have nothing
better to do.

The portions are huge,
but there's nothing to eat.
Everything's salty,
fatty or sweet.

The dishes are hot.
The food is cold.
What's that weird smell?
I think it's mold.

You just want the check,
but the waitress is gone.
You ask for the manager.
They don't have one.

When the dinner's over
as you go out the door,
someone says, "That was great.
I could have eaten a lot more!"

The Nanny

There's an intruder in the house.
No, it's not a mouse.
It's the nanny.
I could not have done it without her,
but there's something weird about her,
the nanny.
She's taking care of my daughter,
but the problem is I bought her —
bought the tender loving care,
and when all is said and done,
that's what's there,
and that's the energy,
that's in my house.

Handyman Special

I'm like an old house.
The roof leaks,
and there's water
in my basement.
The floorboards creak,
and my heater works
intermittently.
The faucets drip.
My insulation's shot,
and there's just the faintest smell
of rot
emanating from my back door.

Some days I feel
like I just can't take it any more.
It seems like everything is on the blink,
but my agent thinks
that with a new coat of paint
I might still have
a little curb appeal.
After all I'm arguably
one of the better houses
on the street,
and there's always somebody
out there who might do a deal.

Waiting

For the phone to ring
For the text to tone
For deliverance
For your safe return
home.

JOE WENKE is a writer, social critic and LGBTQ rights activist. He is the founder and publisher of Trans Über, a publishing company with a focus on promoting LGBTQ rights, free thought and equality for all people. In addition to FREE AIR, Wenke is the author of THE TALK SHOW, a Novel; PAPAL BULL: An Ex-Catholic Calls Out the Catholic Church; YOU GOT TO BE KIDDING! A Radical Satire of The Bible; MAILER'S AMERICA; and THE HUMAN AGENDA: Conversations about Sexual Orientation and Gender Identity, which will be published in January 2015. Wenke received a B.A. in English from the University of Notre Dame, an M.A. in English from Penn State and a Ph.D. in English from the University of Connecticut.

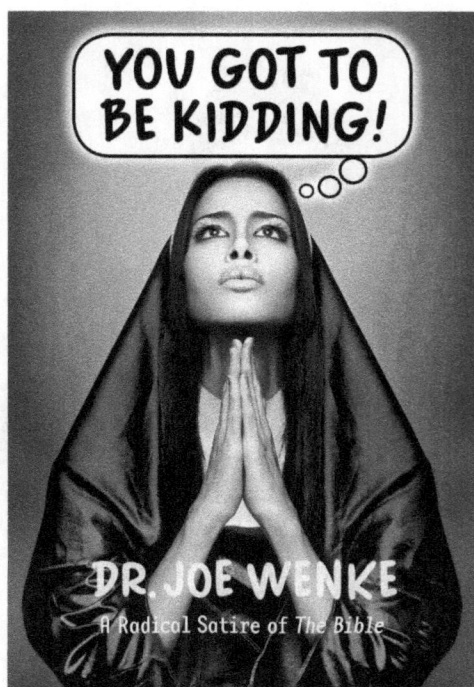

YOU GOT TO
BE KIDDING!

DR. JOE WENKE

A Radical Satire of The Bible

"A radically funny book." *Christopher Rudolph, The Advocate*

"Gisele, the notable transgender fashion model, graces the cover. And that image alone challenges the Bible. A transgender woman in a religious pose. . . . Get [You Got to be Kidding!] on your Kindle or take it on a trip, the time will fly by—boring this is not!" *Transgenderzone*

"A riotously funny read, I recommend it to anyone who's ever questioned organised religion, especially that of the Bible-bashing, homophobic kind." *Anna, Look!*

"This is hilarious! Joe Wenke gives a nod to Mark Twain as he looks at the Bible with fresh eyes and with the pen of a thinking comic." *Bill Baker*

"This is without a doubt the funniest book I've ever read. I sat with my parents and read aloud some of the passages and we all laughed a lot!" *Emma Charlton, Bookswithemma*

"Very tongue-in-cheek, sarcastic and pointed, dedicated to Christopher Hitchens and Thomas Paine, both of whom would, I believe, really enjoy this book!" *Sarah Hulcey*

"The cover of the book itself is a slap in the face of transphobia. . . . If this book accomplishes one thing, I hope it pushes prejudiced people toward acceptance of LGBT people just as they are." *Isaac James Baker, Reading, Writing & Wine*

"Brave, brilliant and funny. Page after page, biblical chapter after biblical chapter, absurdity after absurdity, this book delivers laugh after laugh. Joe Wenke has crafted the answer to the fundamentalist literal reading of the Bible with the perfect recipe of rationality, candor and humor." *Max Gelt*

"Brilliant . . . for once a funny look at ALL the Bible's insanity." *Jo Bryant*

"Would make a really wicked Christmas present for your Christian friends who have a sense of humor and a sense of the ridiculous." *Ed Buckner, American Atheists*

"Oh my! This is very funny . . . Joe turns everything on its head and makes it a really interesting read." *Stephen Ormsby*

"Whether you are an atheist or a Christian who can see the absurdity of some of the anecdotes narrated in Holy Scripture, Joe Wenke's humor won't be wasted on you." *Mina's Bookshelf*

"Great book! Funny and easy to read." *Violets and Tulips*

"Funny and to the point read. Takes a look at the Bible and points out all sorts of inaccuracies, illogical stories and questions. Strongly recommend." *Hertzey*

"Witty and wise. Joe Wenke takes a critical, provocative look at The Bible and he does so with regular hilarity." *Dana Hislop*

"A must-read for anyone who still thinks the Bible is the inviolable word of God—sense of humor mandatory." *K. Sozaeva*

"Such a funny read, my son & I actually read it together! Laughter abounds!" *Rael*

"Deliciously witty!" *Jack Scott*

"Irreverent and hilarious. I am no Bible scholar, but I feel like I have been given the funniest crib notes on this most widely read and probably as widely misunderstood book of all time. I laughed out loud at Wenke's common sense observations and interpretations of this tome." *Lorna Lee*

"Will keep any freethinking reader laughing the whole way through." *George Lichman*

"[You Got to Be Kidding is] entertaining and enlightening." *Patti Bray*

"You will be laughing yourself silly while reading this book! In fact, you may find yourself bookmarking a bunch of pages to discuss with your pastor and friends later!" *S. Henke*

"I could not put this book down." *Jackie Hepton*

"This author allows the reader to explore and learn about the Bible with a tongue-in-cheek attitude that keeps you laughing and turning the pages." *Tricia Schneider*

"Some of it made me feel like I might wind up in hell for reading it, but if you keep an open mind and a light heart, you'll have a blast." *Jon Yost*

"Don't read the Bible! Read this!" *Dr. Dan*

Papal Bull

Dr. Joe Wenke
An Ex-Catholic Calls Out the Catholic Church

ACCLAIM FOR DR. JOE WENKE'S PAPAL BULL

"Joe Wenke is an extraordinary writer. . . . This book is an enlightening journey (for both the author and the reader) that was tenderly written by an exceptional person who is not afraid to let others know about what occurs in so many families, causing a great deal of pain and uncertainty. It is something that should be read by anyone and everyone, regardless of their religion or how they were raised/told by others to believe. There are no words to express the depth of my gratitude to Mr. Wenke and I will be anxiously awaiting any other material that he wishes to write, because I am a lifelong fan." *Jules*

"I may burn in hell for even having read this book." *John C. Wood*

"If you enjoyed Wenke's take on the Bible, You Got to Be Kidding! read his exegesis of the Catholic Church's past two thousand years. . . . Mordantly funny, scrupulously researched." *E. B. Boatner, Lavender Magazine*

"If you wonder why a 'merciful' God created a no-exit-ever hell or if you entertain thoughts of how boring the traditional religious notion of heaven might be, you will meet a savagely witty ally in Wenke's book." *Joe Meyers, CTPost*

"I absolutely LOVED this book. . . . I highly recommend it to any Catholic who is considering recovering from his condition." *Philip G. Harding*

"Ex-Catholics will love this book. It is an amazing satire of the Catholic Church. Every bit as funny as You Got To Be Kidding! I highly recommend." *Holly Michele*

"I love this book! It is not only informative but funny as hell." *Rick Martin*

"Funny, clever and spot on." *V. Kennedy*

"Whew! I feel like I've been to confession with the universe, (not God, that's a bad fairytale) and I've been absolved of . . . something. Thank you, Dr. Wenke, for putting into words . . . what I've been thinking about religion, especially Catholicism for a long time. . . . The one thought that kept repeating for me throughout the book, was that I need to buy about 2 dozen copies of this and hand them out to my family members, and at least try to spark a conversation." *Deborah*

"Papal Bull is brilliant and funny, well-researched and informative. . . . [Dr. Wenke] writes with humor that is at once scathing, insightful and absurd. His recounting of stories from Catholic grade school made me laugh out loud." *Lori Giampa*

"A cutting, satirical look at Catholic beliefs regarding saints, Mary, birth control, the treatment of women, and of course the huge scandalous cover-up of molestation." *Tiffany A. Harkleroad*

"Impeccably researched and sharply written. . . . [Dr. Wenke's] wit and incisive perspective consistently deliver humor and important points to anyone willing to open their minds. . . . A work in which you can think, laugh, and ask the important questions is a must-read." *David Nor*

"For some reason, I kept falling into a George Carlin voice as I read the book." *Joseph Spuckler*

"I love the cover and I love the term 'recovering Catholic' of which I believe I am one. I think any one who went to Catholic School in the fifties and sixties . . . probably had many of the same experiences that the author describes from his school years." *Diane Scholl*

A great and sometimes funny book all 'recovering Catholics' should read. In fact it should be required reading for anybody who considers themselves Holy. Brilliant insight & questions every Catholic should ask themselves." *Robert Kennemer*

"It is necessary to call the church out on their horrendous errors and this book is much needed in society. . . . Papal Bull is timely and makes for some very interesting reading. Enjoy!" *Lynda Smock*

"I not only laughed a great deal, but [the book] also gave me a lot to think about." *Michele Barbrow*

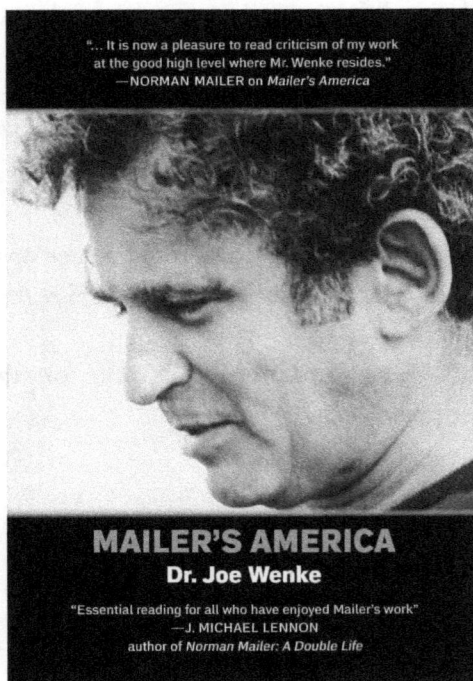

"... It is now a pleasure to read criticism of my work at the good high level where Mr. Wenke resides."
—NORMAN MAILER on *Mailer's America*

MAILER'S AMERICA
Dr. Joe Wenke

"Essential reading for all who have enjoyed Mailer's work"
—J. MICHAEL LENNON
author of *Norman Mailer: A Double Life*

ACCLAIM FOR DR. JOE WENKE'S MAILER'S AMERICA

The reissue of Joseph Wenke's thoughtful study, *Mailer's America*, provides renewed hope for a deeper understanding of Mailer's work. No other commentator has focused so relentlessly on the deepest purpose of Mailer's hugely varied oeuvre, namely to "clarify a nation's vision of itself." Wenke's examination inhabits, patrols and maps the territory between the millennial promise of America and its often dispiriting actuality. His study contains probing, nuanced and careful examinations of all Mailer's work though the mid-1980s, including one of the first major examinations of Mailer's most demanding novel, *Ancient Evenings*. Wenke's book deserves a wide audience, and is essential reading for all who have enjoyed Mailer's work.—*J. Michael Lennon, author of the authorized biography, Norman Mailer: A Double Life*

www.ingramcontent.com/pod-product-compliance
Lightning Source LLC
Chambersburg PA
CBHW020517030426
42337CB00011B/426